This book belongs to:

_____

Pop-Pop Loves Me!

Pop-Pop

Loves me All the time!

We have fun, in the sunshine!

We love to explore things big and small

When we sing songs,
it is a ball!

Pop-Pop

IS ALWAYS UP FOR FUN!

ESPECIALLY IN THE
WARMTH OF THE SUN!

He helps me when there is something I cannot find

He sometimes likes
to take a nap . . .

After that, we learn to use the hammer...
tap, Tap, Tap!

His big hugs can
keep me warm!

Even in a big snow storm

WE ALWAYS EAT THE
VERY BEST TREATS!

We love to hike
and hold
hands...
That is very
sweet!

WE USE OUR IMAGINATION
WHEN WE PLAY.

We Play ball and grill together

during the day.

Pop-Pop

Loves to watch me GROW!

HE LOVES TO SEE

HOW MUCH

I KNOW!

I KNOW HE LOVES ME EVERY DAY... EVEN IF HE IS FAR AWAY.

I WISH WE COULD PLAY...
EVERY DAY!

I LOVE HIM...
WE ALWAYS HAVE FUN!
SOMETIMES I AM SAD WHEN
OUR DAY IS DONE.

Made in the USA
Columbia, SC
01 December 2024

48112211R00020